THE PUPPET MAN
New & Selected Poems

THE PUPPET MAN
New & Selected Poems

Don Wallis

The Hutton Street Press
San Luis Obispo, California
2014

Copyright © 2014 by Don Wallis

Cover art: Don Wallis, *Self Portrait*, 2004
Author photo: Einar Berg

All rights reserved. This book or any portion thereof may not be reproduced or used in any manner whatsoever without the express written permission of the publisher except for the use of brief quotations in a book review or scholarly journal.

First Printing: August 2014

ISBN 978-0-692-26474-4

The Hutton Street Press
Mission Station
Post Office Box 15552
San Luis Obispo, CA 93406

Website: www.donwallis.com
Email: don@donwallis.com

These poems are dedicated to my family

Bob, Emma, Milo & John

CONTENTS

Acknowledgements ix

i

The Puppet Man 13
The Lions and The Lambs 15
When I Think of My Father 17
Singing Other People's Songs 18
Poetry and Art 20
A Movie in My Head 23
The Actors 25
Thoughts in A Wooden Head 28
Dawn Near The Water 29
Dreams 31
Geppetto in America 33
Farmers Market Puppeteer 35

ii

The Asian Classics 39
The Dream 40
Top Secret 41
Thomas 42
My Parents 44
Vincent 45
Boris Pasternak 47
I, Mayakovsky 49
General Custer and The Long Three Martini Lunch 53

The End of Us 55
Exploding Birds 58
A Public Prayer 61
A Thank You Note to Ferlinghetti 62
My Mentor, Rafael 64

iii

One Night When I Was Little 69
An Early Education 71
My Alternative Service 73
Notes for Another WWII Movie 75
Korean War Vet 78
Bicycling California 79
The Wedding 81
Sergei Obraztsov 83
Winter Music in Yosemite 84
The Eldest Son 85
Day of The Dead 87
Fathers & Sons 89
My Arrival in Paris 92
Spartacus 94
A Fine Tune 95
My Labors and Wages 96

ACKNOWLEDGEMENTS

I gratefully acknowledge the editors of the journal *Poets & Paupers* for publishing "Boris Pasternak" in the 1990s; and I thank the editors at DeerTree Press for publishing "Thomas" in *Corners Of The Mouth A Celebration Of Thirty Years At The Annual San Luis Obispo Poetry Festival* in 2014.

I thank Einar Berg, Beverly Boyd, Ivan Brownotter, Russell Bunge, Kevin & Amy Clark, Lisa Coffman, Evelyn Cole, Mike Cowdrey, James Cushing, Ray Clark Dickson, Marysha Maziarz Dickson, Celeste Goyer, Ken Hall, Ben Lawless, Sue McGintey, Jack Mothershed, David Neubauer, David Ochs, Jerry Smith, Dian Sousa and Kevin & Patti Sullivan for their kindness; and I thank you the reader.

i

THE PUPPET MAN

    1.
I stand before an audience
And wrinkle my face
Like a capuchin monkey.
The insides of my eyebrows
Angle upward. Then I start
To sigh and everyone laughs
And gets the giggles.

    2.
I hold my puppets
Wolfie and Red Riding Hood
Up because they're little.
Hansel and Gretel
Smile at strangers.
They wave and cheer
In high-pitched voices.
And a lot of friendly people
Look up and wave back.
Don Quixote attacks a windmill
And Sancho Panza shakes his head
Becoming more and more frustrated.
Each has their own mind and heart.
Each thinks and feels.
The hero. The villain.
I play both roles at the same time.
And I let them act, and react,
Until I get all warmed up in the heart,
Elated, and worn down in the head
So the smaller children
And the larger people in their families
Can see themselves, and each other:
How they wonder, and dream,

And how they look when they feel joy
And laugh. I even get them
To throw their arms high into the air
Screaming "Yea!" like small
Monkeys themselves leaping
From branch to branch through the trees
Acting like they're alive

THE LIONS AND THE LAMBS

I imagine cuts
On a poor boy's feet
As he climbs, foot by foot,
Hand over hand, up a cliff
On the coast of Cyprus,
Bouncing up out of each new
Wave that slams him
Thin against the rocks:
Tanned body, curly hair, white teeth.
I want to talk to him
About what I heard
About children missing legs
Who survived land mines.
One in a hospital bed
On a t.v. program last year
When we visited my cousins
Sang a song about a bluebird
With joy in his voice
And maybe in his heart
And a smile on his face
Without even a trace
Of him being hurt.

I've read in a crumpled up
National Geographic—
How little girls in Haiti
And Brazil hunt, rain or shine,
Through mountains of garbage
To find food scraps
To feed themselves
And their little brothers
And their tiny dogs.
I've heard about young girls
Being raped in brothels

And boys smaller than me
Being forced to kill grown-ups
And other children with rifles
And machetes.

I go to school.
I've got three books:
Arithmetic, Stories and Geography.
I think I'll get another
Classics Illustrated comic book:
Genghis Khan, *The Red Badge
Of Courage* or *Moby Dick*
The next time Mom says
I can go to town with Dad
In the pickup.

I picture the deep black
And milk-white eyes
Of an Incan girl leading
A llama carrying a bundle
Of frozen sticks
Up a high Andean road.
Her long bold braids
Rock back and forth
Through her steaming breath
In the glacial air
And I want to ask her things
Like if she thinks
There're kids all over the world
Pretending to play soccer
With a real ball
Instead of a tin can
Or a clod of dirt
And whether or not one
Might be wondering if
There's still a kid like them
In California somewhere.

WHEN I THINK OF MY FATHER

My body warms up
And I become passive, weak
And vulnerable
When I think of you, Dad,
Because you were God
In the world we held
And not just a hero or a priest.
And I wish I could see you
And touch you
And have you hold me
One more time, and then let me die
In your arms and go to sleep forever
So I would never
Have to miss you again.
Just feel myself in your lap
For as long as I lived.

SINGING OTHER PEOPLE'S SONGS

Dad and I sang together
In the 1950s: songs he learned
From hobos in the 1930s
And tunes written by
The young Johnny Cash.
I tried to sound like a grown-up.
I raised my voice and deepened it
Until I coughed and had to clear
My throat before I started choking.

I remember sliding my left hand
Down the soft nylon strings
On the neck of my Mexican folk guitar
And hammering with my fingertips
To form the notes.
I hounded the ears and souls
Of my audience howling Bob Dylan's
"The Times They Are A-Changin."
I sang my throat raw,
Wanting to keen, like Phil Ochs strumming
His acoustic steel-stringed guitar hard
And singing "So I Guess
I'll Have To Do It While I'm Here"
High and higher. I wanted
To sing like the British John Lennon
Humming his prayerful lullaby "Imagine"
To console and offer hope
To all the people
Falling asleep in the world.
I sang along to The Jefferson Airplane
And The Rolling Stones
Before the speed in the 60s changed
The sound of all the screaming
Among the notes. It became

Painful. Everything
From my lips to my brain trembled.

But I sang. I belted out
Everything from the chants
In the Greek tragedies of Euripides
To all the Irish ballads
About good ol' Boys and Lasses
And their untimely deaths.
I settled for singing other people's songs.
I sang more solos than duets;
And now I wonder what my dad thought—
How he felt—when he sang alone
And when we sang together…
And if there was a difference.

POETRY AND ART

    1.
Some children see sunlight
Shining through water drops
Hanging on their eyelashes
When they wake up in the morning
And start to become aware
Of themselves as they begin
To see the things around them.
Some babies in diapers
Grab at dandelions
And chase butterflies
Like the bald and bare-faced monk,
Thomas Merton, running around
With his camera, tripping
On his cassock and falling
With a full moon glowing
All over his grinning face.
And some teenagers go dancing
With their partners: twirling them like
The curly haired painter Marc Chagall
Holding a white wedding dress
As it disappears out of his arms
Like a cloud into vapor,
Like breath, high in the sky,
While the green and yellow head
Of a bull moos sweet alfalfa lyrics
To a blue and white cow.

    2.
Who but a tiny girl
Would want to pour bottled water
On the damp sand at the edge of a beach
To muddy it enough to squish
Between her toes and fingers…

As if she were planting her thoughts
And feelings inside her and
Deepening her body into the ground?
Who but a girl
Would dream of being
On her grandmother's farm
And standing beside her
While she sat on a cracked-oak stool
Milking a cow—and want to show her
How she, too, could dip her hand
Into a pail of cream
And let the baby calf lick the milk
Off her fingers? And who
But a teenage Cinderella
Would try to survive seven years
Of grief by hunting
The shelves of literature
To touch the wild animals
In the poems of Elizabeth Bishop
Or dusting the cobwebbed walls
Of art history to be held
By the paintings of Mary Cassatt?

      3.
I'm still a two year old boy
Out searching for sourgrass
Lost in a pasture of weeds.
And I'm with the others crouching
Among gargoyles overlooking
The Hunchback of Notre Dame.
Boys hang from trees.
They throw tantrums like gorillas
Caged in cardboard boxes
And kick telephone poles
Like martyrs being crucified all down
The sidewalks on their block.
Some days I'm afraid and a coward

With a long day ahead to think…
And who but the other boys
Like Tolstoy would climb up on a tractor
To greet another sunrise
And plow the earth until it sets…
Or like Hemingway
Would squeeze their Teddy Bear
One last time before
They crawled up out of a trench
To face a bullet or a bayonet?
And some like Homer and Goya
Stare directly into the sun,
Or at the moon,
Long enough to go blind.

A MOVIE IN MY HEAD

Wandering out of the Haight,
I stepped off the curb
Into a cumulus cloud
Somewhere over an intersection
In San Francisco. And,
As I rose, I heard the people
On the sidewalks screaming
Through the brilliance of the light.
I lost my breath.
I rolled my shoulders back
And raised my eyes
Into the illuminated sky
Over the Pacific… and the thought
Came to me that I might be
A bomber pilot flying away
From Hiroshima or Nagasaki.
I became afraid I might see
Bodies of well-behaved children
Who needed doctors and nurses
And bandages and blood
Trying to walk, or crawl,
Across the dust and ashes
Among the clouds around me.
So I closed my eyes
And really wondered who
But the land or the ocean
Would hold any of these children,
Wipe their tears, hum them songs
And promise them they would
Never be harmed again… and,
Squinting my eyes real tight,
I saw them
Playing most attentively
And some were trying to get the adults

In their families and neighborhoods
To stop what they were doing
And join them and
Those who did started smiling…
And I shivered, feeling
My eyes and nostrils opening
Among the sweet-smelling
Cherry tree blossoms between me
And a full moon outside Kyoto…
But my screen went blank,
My projector unwound my color film
On the street and the screams
I had first heard on the set,
Finally, became the voice
Of a lovely young mother
In Korea or Vietnam humming
A lullaby to her child.

THE ACTORS

for Einar Berg

I remember seeing
An actor fall flat on a stage
And start to swim
Like a Bluefin tuna in the Atlantic
And all of us in the house
Smelled the brine,
Tasted the salt and felt
His fins against our eyes;
And then he stood up
And raised his arm over his head
To become a hangman's rope
Tightening around his neck
And all of us jumped
And dangled from the horror
Trapped in our throats and stomachs
And kicked to stay alive.

An actor trusts a playwright—
That the actions of his characters
Are mapped and plotted
Over the course of a play.
He trusts himself
To discover the steps he will take
As he faces
Each moment and watches
And listens and then reacts
Before he speaks. And
Trusts his director
Will help him feel safer
On the journey as
He learns to be on time
To enter again into the light
Moving out of the darkness—

How to walk, to talk—
And when to exit, when
To close the curtain and how
To bring down the house.

The theater has always
Been a place where men
Could express their feelings;
And some young
Men need to do that
More than others.
And some of us have
Lived in this house
Nearly all our lives.

Einar worked with Al Pacino.
He wanted to play with James Dean.
We almost played Steinbeck's
George and Lenny—
Almost packed the gun,
And used it, and bothered everyone
About the rabbits… but
I played Jekyll and Hyde.
And Einar dared to listen
To my voice and look me
In the eyes. We talked
Over coffee, elbow to elbow,
At a table outside a donut
Shop near the theater
Where he was playing Quixote
And hearing the applause
Of audiences, taking encores
And getting hugs from
The cast and crew backstage.
We talked about the character
John Muir in the Sierras—
Talked about walking

Through a valley of flowers
To smell them and to breathe,
And a most beautiful
Providence in life—
In all wildness—
In all death…
Long after we played Shakespeare's
Banquo and Macbeth
On their way to their graves.

THOUGHTS IN A WOODEN HEAD

*"Wood's alive until it petrifies,
and maybe even longer."*

The grandson of woodsmen and farmers,
I used to wander in the forest
For hours in the shade…
Breathing air from the leaves
On hundreds of trees. And now
I haven't been out in days.
I feel the warmth of the wide chisel
Smooth the basswood
As I carefully move my arms
And take another slip away
From this small head
And little pair of hands.
This puppet won't follow
The Pied Piper of Hamelin.
He'll be innocent, and wise.
He'll love having heart-to-hearts
With people and laughing with children.
And, by the way he's smiling already,
He'll practice kindness and hope
All the years he lives.
I'll turn folk tales into plays
And perform them with him.
I'll prune each gesture and word
To incite the audiences
To feel and think well enough
To protect themselves
From any villain here
Who tries to harm them.
Oh, Little Boy, I'm
In such a big hurry
I'll stop for a while this evening
Or tomorrow morning and we'll play.

DAWN NEAR THE WATER

     1.
Geese and ducks fly fast across the river.
I hear their laughter
Coming off the ripples in the water.
The sun breaks through the wet fog
Between my eyes and the horizon
And I remember the chill inside me
I associate with you,
The one I felt when I watched
You raise your slender thumb
And long, elongated fingers…
Blue and white.

     2.
I sense you move in every breeze—
I feel you when the still air
Shifts its weight. These things
Remind me that you did soften
When you were happy like
When you looked at tea-dyed lace…
Or fondly touched crochet the way
Your fingertips used to brush up
Against my hair, pat my chin
Or use a warm damp cloth
To wash the sticky stuff
Off the tiny palms and fingers
Of my little hands.

     3.
I now prefer to see
Your presence in a young girl's face
Or in a small child's eyes
Than to see your absence
Near a lilac scarf hanging down

The front of a mirror or draped
Over the back of an empty chair.

    4.
Now I can't touch you.
I can't respond with my voice,
My face, my hands.
I've lost your ears, your lips,
Your eyes, your fingertips…
I want to ask you things
And only the air all around me
Tells me where I am,
What I am and who…
I'm cold. I am so cold.
And I'm still afraid I might freeze, too,
And stick to the ice
I saw you buried in.

DREAMS

I still want to look
Into Buddha's eyes
And see Moses crying with joy
When he finally gets to see
Jesus pulling Peter and Judas
In close to Him, telling jokes,
At the Marriage of Cana
While they're drinking the wine.
I want to enter an oasis
In the desert
And kneel with Mohammed
To pray to Allah to thank Him
For all the water
I have already been given
In my life… and for the bread,
And the dates and the prayers.
I want to float on my back
On the Ganges under the stars
And inhale a mouthful of smoke
From Gandhi's ashes
To get close enough to Him
To tell Him something funny
So I can see His huge big grin again
And His one little tooth.

I want to have enough faith
To enter a Delivery Room
And hold my first child
And know that for her whole life
She, or he, will be all-right.
Happy, even. And fulfilled.
I want to live until the very air
That holds me up lays me down

And the breath of God
leaves my mouth, my tongue
And my lips.

GEPPETTO IN AMERICA

I lean on my workbench.
I strain to hold my thoughts
And my mallet.
I used to remember names,
Knew where my friends
Lived in the forest
And which of them were still alive.
Dazed, I stare at the pine dolls
And popguns I still have
To carve, paint and wrap
In the colorful comic pages
Of the Sunday newspapers.
The room around me's darkened
As my eyesight's dimmed.
And all the things in it
Move faster now than they did.
The templates. The tools.
Critical, and scared…
Forgetful. I'm so sleepy,
I criticize myself
For being so tired
I could cut myself with a chisel.
There have been days, even lately,
When I smiled in the heat
Still coming to the planet,
Knowing roots and leaves
Were growing all over the world
And I saw, and felt,
Little breezes lifting rainbows
Out of the dew on hillsides
And stirring the petals
In the flower beds
Out in the yards…
When I raised my eyes

And saw, and appreciated,
The air carrying butterflies
And large fluffy white clouds.
But today I feel
Like my mind, body and soul
Are hollow and spreading apart…
My thoughts are like driftwood,
Or petrified seaweed, and my memories
Float in and out along my mind
Looking for nothing, nothing at all.
And the palm tree outside
My window's shaking
In the hot Santa Ana winds
Like it's nearly lashing the shed
Or going to smash one of
The neighborhood children in the head.
Wind's coming. Real wind.

FARMERS MARKET PUPPETEER

I'm sore after packing
My booth and puppets back into the car.
I move with the heavy shoulders
Of an old farmer in the evening
Following some cows home to the barn.
I know already tonight
I'll wander over my memories
Like an ancient Greek
At an outdoor theater:
So many heart-to-hearts
And smiles listed in columns
Like bushels of wheat
And boxes of grapes...

I'm tired but I've time
Like I did in the beginning
When I started to face my fears
By standing and performing
With puppets on my hands
In public to children.
And families started trusting me
To get their kids laughing,
And they did so hard
They got the giggles
And some of the adults
And older kids joined in
And we felt our feelings rush
Through us as we booed villains
And tingled, and yelled to heroes
And warmed, and stretched
Our abilities maybe
A little more to give and take,
And share... so tomorrow
When we arrive in the garden

For the planting we'll see
We won't harm ourselves
Or our neighbors or
Anyone else living far away…
And then we'll meet again
In the market, in the street,
To distribute the harvest among
Everyone because even in the dark
Of our unlit places,
Whether it's dimming eyesight
Or just a dream, we'll
Still see 3 billion children
Standing up and screaming
At life, ourselves and me
To not be so selfish
Or competitive… or stooped
Under the weight of things.

ii

THE ASIAN CLASSICS
to Kenneth Rexroth

I'm waiting out a rainstorm at a counter in an
all-night cafe.
   Teamsters and ranchers on my right talk with
a middle-aged waitress pouring coffee like
they're all combat veterans of both World Wars
and Korea.
   I re-open your New Directions paperback.
   I remember an old Chinese poet you
translated said, "Life and youth are more
special than a young person realizes...
and our hearts are the center of our minds..."
I look to my left out the window. I see the
residue light from the few neon signs in the dark
windows of the bar across the street; and I think
of the line "maidens in feudal Japan rushing
with monks and scholars over a bridge,
giggling, on their way back from a lake, trying
to outrun the rain."
   I remember the cherry tree blossoms at the
Japanese Tea Garden in San Francisco last
Spring. My friends eyes brightened then
among the pink little petals that are so pretty
in the sunlight after a shower before they drop
and fade like the discarded words of a soggy
newspaper. My friends are now eighteen.
One's headed for Nam, another to Canada and
the third to prison. I'm seventeen. And,
reminded who I am, I close your book again
and reach for a napkin and my pen and for the
first real time in my life I begin to write about
the warmth inside me, too, and about the chill
in the air outside.

THE DREAM

My mind's green with icebergs
Bumping each other on the North Sea…
As I drag my pillow
Like a polar bear across
The creaking wooden floor,
Through the crack in the doorway
And out into the shimmering light
Down the hall. Dad's
Standing in a shadow, waiting.
"Where are you going?" He asks.
"I don't know," I say.
Everything's gray,
And turning darker,
Except the lights…
I'm paddling a kayak
Through the streamers
Of the Aurora Borealis
To find the Vikings
On the serpent ship
To show them my polar bear

TOP SECRET

My parents would never admit
They dropped depth charges into the dark
Or that they helped float mines
In the silence in this world…
So I'm still hiding
In the shadows in my closet
Fingering the button eyes
Of my soggy stuffed animal,
Too afraid to talk,
Watching their eyes and lips
Drift away like life jackets
And rubber rafts as they say again,
"Don't be afraid…"
and tears flood my lungs
and my heart starts to float
like a drowned man's body
in a submarine.

THOMAS

Gethsemane was hard.
I was so tired of doubting
Myself and you, I slept.
And through the days of
Your arrest, the trial and the cross
I started doubting
Everything you had said.
I need to touch things
And weigh them like
A fisherman does his catch…
Or a man hugs his friend.
I'm grabbing men
And turning them around
And shaking them and lifting
Their robes and sleeves and looking
To see if they have your scars
And wounds. And they don't.
They have their own.
I'm going blind looking
For your face; and deaf
Listening for your voice.
It's like I see the darkness
Shining with beings of light
Beyond the stars—
And you entering the room
Like sunshine through an open roof…
And you're like the sunlight
Through the morning mist
On the Sea of Galilee
Singing after a rain.
Master, how can I believe
Our Father is our dad:
That he is present, is eternal,
Is life itself—and that he guides us

When I don't know
If you're alive or dead?

MY PARENTS

Dad and mom served
To win the war.
They held to truths
They had been taught as children
As if their minds were in their hands
And their hearts were in their fingers.
And they prayed in silence.
And when the victory celebrations ended
They folded their bodies up:
He in a tavern, she in a kitchen…
And they prayed some more
To convince themselves
That they really had saved
The world from evil…
And then they prayed even harder
When I and the rest of my generation
Had to be spanked, beaten and jailed
When we got in their faces and started
Asking the truth from everyone.

VINCENT

*for the poorest of the poor
still in our world.*

Ramon leaned toward me and whispered, "The sound of this world eating people is an awful sound, isn't it? Van Gogh was a painter. He painted life as he saw it in the lives of peasants, in their working places, in their shacks, in their bodies, and he painted it. He painted life moving. He painted life and none of his paintings bought him even the littlest piece of cheese or bread. His work wasn't as valuable as money. So, Van Gogh was very thin and hungry. Ah, there was so much pain in him. But he wanted to live. He had work to do. A field of corn. He raised his brush. He started painting. The heat of the sun seared his eyes and the inside of his skull. A genius—and a field of corn right there in front of him. He had it almost finished. Then a flock of loud cawing crows flew down into the golden tassels on the corn and started devouring it. Van Gogh hears and sees them spoiling what he needed to paint. All of it. All over the field. The world. Oh, the noise, and the sight of it: the crows gobbling and gobbling. It killed him. The world and the crows, of course, refusing to take the blame called it suicide because first he slashed off his ear to be rid of the noise and then he pulled the pistol's trigger with the same fingers he had used to paint."

"Ah, I'm whispering," Ramon said. "I'm whispering so very softly, aren't I? This world made a valuable commodity out of Van Gogh and all of his work after he died. Influential people made him a famous man. They raised the value of his paintings to a price that only the richest could afford. How about that? Nothing changes, does it?"

    Ramon stared at the sky and said, "He painted the crows in first though, didn't he?"

BORIS PASTERNAK

*Nobel Prize Winner
for Literature, 1958*

His face looked like the head of an Arabian horse and it wasn't difficult to imagine him shaking and jerking in the thick, heavy winds whirling round the golden church domes and wheat fields in Russia.

1914: mankind was sick. Everyone was hungry. Even the richest households had turned from caviar and champagne to beets and onions. Europeans shot their own countrymen; and twenty-some years later they did it again. Children made slingshots. The smallest threw rocks. Millions of handfuls of dirt seeped through mourners' fingers and fell on coffin lids, boards, planks... Husbands. Sons. Brothers. Fathers. Packed into holes in the ground.

And Boris felt it. He empathized with other people who were struggling and starving enough to write: "Life resurrects the fragrance of pollinated tassels of corn." And his verse became seeds for the Russian soul, the only hard things he ever threw at the world.

Oh... His mother had given concerts, playing Scriabin on the classical piano; and his father had done art, painting their friend Tolstoy in oils. But Boris wrote poetry, a novel and translated Shakespeare into modern Russian. He saved the lives of hundreds of friends, acquaintances and strangers when Joseph Stalin phoned in the middle of the night to check on their loyalty and obedience. But he failed to save the life of one of the best ones, his friend, the poet Osip Mandelstam and he had to control himself and the tone in his voice for the rest of the conversation to defend so many others. That's bravery; that's heroism. That's absolute madness and he did it: with his face shaped like the head of an Arabian horse snorting wildly in the wind breathing the air between the grains of sand, windstorms all around him, across the steppes at full gallop.

I, MAYAKOVSKY

A warning to the West.

I've shot myself, Maria.
Roulette. I played with a bullet
In a revolver
As a metaphor, maybe,
For the violent madness in life.

I wanted to share my words
The way I thought a Siberian peasant
Would share his last borscht,
And onion and potato
On the coldest day in winter
With his comrades in a prison camp…
So I wrote my epic about
My relationship with the workers,
The soldiers, the people.

I traveled
From battlefield to battlefield,
City to city…
Trying to inspire the workers
To master themselves
And break their chains.

I praised our progress.
I praised me.
I drank. I danced
In a marvelous factory—
Even my teeth gleamed
Like a nobleman's chandelier.

I was applauded
By tyrants and commissars.
I lived like a prince.

I oppressed a person
Inside me like he
And all the masses on Earth
Were my appropriated serfs,
My personal slaves.

And, now, I'm crawling
Like a wounded bear
Retreating into a Russian forest
Looking for a cave…
Clawing the ground,
Clawing the frozen ice,
Losing my strength
And only finding it
Harder and harder to breathe.

We were lovers, Maria.
Remember the beginning,
Not the end. Maria,
I'm down on all fours
On your carpet. You could
Find me with your feet.
Grab me around the neck.
Pull me up into your bed.
Press your palms against my cheeks
And kiss me on my lips.

Let me shout.
Let me talk.
Let me say something about all men—
If not to you—if not to someone—
Then to a night star
Above the fog thickening over me
Like a blanket
As I end my prayers
And fall asleep.
I dreamed of love

My whole life…
While I worked for fame
Like a vulture
In search of dead flesh
Pecking the world with its beak to live.
I became the revolutionary—
The poet—in this holiest of lands;
So, it's my own fault.
I raised the pistol
And pulled the trigger
With my own hand.

Should I hang myself;
Have I made enough enemies
To get lynched?
My breath is blinding my eyes;
My limbs and claws
Are freezing to the ice.
Who cares?
          I did.
What does it matter?
          I still do.

The rich get profits off numbers
Faster and faster while
The workers, the soldiers, the people
Lose their value altogether.

I imagine heaven, Maria,
Will be a warm room
In a wooden dacha
Where I'll be reading poems
Out loud, roughly, to twelve
Or so intimate friends
Each of us bearing our brows
And cheeks to the light
From a kerosene lamp

As it illuminates the moisture
In our eyes
While snow falls outside
Quieting our minds…
And we drink vodka
And sing our hearts out, Maria,
Like worn out saints
To recover our strength
And rekindle the glow
To our halos and our souls

GENERAL CUSTER AND
THE LONG THREE MARTINI LUNCH

after Arthur Miller
& Ernest Hemingway

I'm surrounded by White men
And everyone's shooting…
But I'm here to sell Sitting Bull
The rights to hunt buffalo
On the far side of the moon;
And so I'm drinking a little more
Than usual to close the deal.

Any of my associates
Could have gotten lost and frostbit
As I did last winter
Walking door-to-door
Without the proper ammunition
And footwear in a snowstorm
In Vermont, or Alaska.

There's always the current quarter
And the newest line of hunting rifles—
And fishing tackle.
But it's never the product.
It's the man.

I'm thawing on this bar
Like a cut of meat on a butcher tray
In a stainless steel kitchen,
Trembling before the sizzling grill…
Awaiting to be burned for another meal
At a formal banquet in the morgue.

And the air and water in my blood
Rises like ocean mist into the clouds…

And runs like the streams
In the mountains toward
The busy mouths of trout and salmon
And the biting gums of their young.

THE END OF US

I step forward
Through the dark surrounding me
In the dry air of the Vatican.
I sense my right foot is numb.
The left one, too.
Approaching Pope John XXIII,
A country priest
Who usually smiles and laughs
Like my grandmother,
I see he is crying.
His tears look pink
In the candlelight of the altar.
I see blood, wine and holy water
Splashing in the gold chalice
He is holding between
The trembling white knuckles
On his puffy fists.

A voice in the shadows
Says, "No.
The pope is John Paul II now."

I genuflect, and kneel.
"Please," I say
To the One in the light and dark
Who I still believe
Is more alive than I am.
I imagine seeing people's tears
Collapsing on their upper lips
And getting stuck between their teeth.
I remember the Kennedys
And Martin Luther King.
I remember Jesus
Sweating blood all night

In the Garden of Gethsemane
And how his bloodstained face
Glowed in the torchlight at dawn
When He grabbed Peter's arm to stop him
From striking any of the men
The authorities had sent to arrest Him.

But that's not appropriate, not now,
Or is it?

The truth is:
I got up early, sat,
And listened to the echoes
Of the crash.
I watched the parts of the planes,
The buildings and the people
Spread apart through the clouds
Of smoke and dust.
I stiffened like the metal
Splinters and the molten glass
Buried among the basements
Of the Twin Towers.
I saw things.
Here a bone in a briefcase,
There a tooth in the melted face
Of a watch.
My mind and heart were
In my stomach.
I hugged my ribs.
I felt like a clod of holy ground
Being dug up to be a cemetery again.
One that was already overused.
My head hurt.
My brain was all wadded up
Like a used sheet of surgical linen,
Drenched in blood
The man-in-a-hurry on television

Kept shouting
Through the gutted windows,
"We've got the most fighter planes
on Earth. Our country's the most
Powerful in the history
Of the world. We've got more
Nuclear warheads and missiles
Than anybody else. Let
All the nations be scared to death."

I realized I loved to see
People breathe and move
More than I liked to see
Anything break and crumble.

"Peace," I said. "Peace."
And I continued praying long after
I felt the weight
Of the light from the altar
Bend my lashes down
Into the tears on my eyes.
And I saw the Blood of Man
Stretching across the horizon
Like a red sunset and then retract
Into the last flicker of Light.

EXPLODING BIRDS

Young American soldiers,
Men and women...
Wearing sunglasses and headphones,
We shoot pigeons
Out of the dark rafters
In the red barns overseas.
Squabs explode
In a 120 degree heat...
All their little pieces
Burning in the humidity...
Pulverized little birds
Splattering their blood,
Sweat and urine on everything.

Maybe we're sunbathing
On a hotel balcony on vacation
Pretending we're
Hans Solo, Indiana Jones
Or Harrison Ford
Overlooking the whole Third World.
Entire populations
Move like scrap bones...
Hobbling across the bridges,
Villages and fields.

More than likely
I'm hallucinating
On a joy-ride in a Humie,
Deaf as a sand dune in a storm.
Maybe we're marching
Among corpses in the desert,
Shuffling... step... step...
Toward images of blindfolds,
Rifle barrels and bullet holes

In the gritty walls of Baghdad…
Maybe we're stepping forward
Through another minefield,
Sweating salt tablets
Out of the back of our minds.

Scrawny Alabama kid
With the Killer For Christ tattoo
Playing with the shotgun over there's
Our squad idiot,
Uncoordinated, slow-witted…
But his girlfriend, sister
And his old mom and dad
Keep phoning to try to tell him
How hard it is for them
To have to wonder about things.
And to worry. And he doesn't
Have a problem understanding that.
Maybe he really doesn't want
To let anyone down.

"Copy that."

I'm imagining I'm St. Francis
Who, once, after a battle in Europe,
Dropped his sword
And lowered his shield.
Got himself wounded. Retreated. AWOL.
Francis would think he needed
The heart to stop trying
To murder any of these other people,
And desert, and go home
To stand trial for treason…
To hold his wounds shut
With his fingernails
And leave the fighting
By walking off this battlefield.

Most of us think
It's sickening to see this
So we don't look.
Some stare.
The whole thing's a mess…
And loud… the helicopters,
The missiles and the bombs.
Sergeant's yelling at us
To get a hard on—
And start burning the pigeon shit
And mite-infested feathers
With flamethrowers.

So, we will.

A PUBLIC PRAYER

I'm standing in Berkeley
And Paris. I'm standing in front
Of the Lincoln Memorial
In Washington, D.C...
And I'm still thinking of myself
As a kid: like the sad James Dean
Turning around in the corner and
Coming out from the back of the class,
Shaking his head, walking up and pointing
His trembling fingers at his teacher.
I can't imagine Martin Luther King
Being this nervous. Even without
People standing beside him
Martin would not be concerned
About his cowardice, but
Only his endurance and his strength.
I'm still trying to be brave.

A THANK YOU NOTE TO FERLINGHETTI

How many dates and names
In the history of art and writing…
How many mornings you must have
Empathized with painters standing
At their easels to paint
What they saw in broad daylight
Like the morning you entered
A village with Camille Pissarro
While you were looking at a painting
He had done back in 1898…
Preparing yourself to stand
Under the hot electric lights of a
Courtroom in San Francisco, maybe,
So Allen Ginsberg could howl
At the Puritans who had started
The fires of hell burning in America.

I heard you read after
People's Park in Berkeley in the 60s.
I remember the riot clubs the police used.
And the shotguns they fired.
And the martial law
And the armed National Guard.
I remember losing my mind.
I've lived 40 years afraid
Of losing it again.
I wondered how your painting was going
As I leaned against a French train window
On my way back
to the Musée d'Orsay in 1996.
I had just seen Van Gogh's crows
Flying to Auvers… and, unable to stop them,
I stayed in my seat and let the sunlight
Claw my head through the glass.

I blinked. I…

Just knowing you have never
Tolerated despair, and that you, too, feel
More than you think, has helped… like
This morning, Lawrence, when I turned
The television off and went for a walk
Across the creek downtown
In the bright sunlight May 24, 2005.

MY MENTOR, RAFAEL

for Rafael Rubenstein

I remember hearing you had died, Rafael.
"Three days ago, Don. He was a
beautiful person," Regina said.
I remember the evening of chamber music:
"a private concert, only a few friends," for
two hours in your home. The flautist, the
violinist, the guy on the French horn from
New York and you, Rafael. You played
Bach on white on black a thousand notes
per minute.
Putting your hand on my arm, you said,
"The violinist Regina, she plays well, yes?"
"She sure does."
"She's vicious. Our egos… together, we
argue. You understand? She's with the Los
Angeles and Santa Barbara symphonies.
Before she was born I performed in Berlin."

…your moustache hanging over your lips.
Your broad forehead wrinkling back. The
firm teeth in your grin.
"Let's drink to Regina. I've always liked
her even though she's a little bit the religious
fanatic. The vodka, more vodka, please."
"Is it Russian?" I asked.
"No," you said a little slowly, showing me
the label. "It's English."

"Rafael, I never asked you to teach me
to laugh down a drink while tears flooded
my stomach… And I never asked you how
to measure the depth of another person's
heart, the temperature of their hands…"

"But, Don, I have. Have another drink."

I remember the night you pounded your knuckles on a round wooden table in the student coffee house on the UCSB campus while, on stage, I strummed mere chords and flubbed the changes. During the break I thanked you for your patience. You clutched the arms of your chair and punched me in the face with your head. "Don't insult me. Don't apologize for simplicity. I love music… simple folk, Russian, African, American. It's all music."
"Bob Dylan said that too, Rafael."
"Good. He's right."
Second set I sang myself hoarse.

I remember us discussing art in front of the paintings in your home. We were eating herring and cheese. I pointed at a portrait. Herring juice dripped down my hand, and there were bits of cheese on my lips, but I had a question to ask.
"Rafael, do you figure someone who painted could capture the feeling of a fella putting food right in the palm of another fella's hands?"
"Aesthetics, hmmm?"
You thought about it as you spread chopped liver on a cracker. "Let's see…" You handed me the cracker. "An artist never captures, an artist is a person who can release."
You looked about the table, I took a bite of liver, and you grinned. "It's good, yes? An artist does not compete with the passing of chopped liver between human beings."

iii

ONE NIGHT WHEN I WAS LITTLE

One night up at the Ranch
When I was pretty drowsy
After a late supper
Of venison and mashed potatoes
And gravy, I rubbed my cheek
Against the grain of the bobcat fur
Hanging over the back
Of my grandfather's chair.
The fur smelled like fresh oats
Coated with warm molasses.
I breathed hard and groaned.
"No more food," I said,
Holding my stomach, and
Massaging it, with my fingers.
Then I heard my grandpa
At the table near the wood burning
Stove in the kitchen say
Something about seasons and
Sacrifice… and dad said something
About young kids dying in the war.
And wondering what they
Were talking about, and why,
I started to wonder
How old things were when they died:
The chair, the bobcat, my parents.
I stared into the lit kerosene lamp
On the nightstand
And imagined the wick
Looked like a honeycomb
And the flame was flowing
Like warm melted honey
As I moved my mind
Through the heat around to
The other side of the lamp

And thought of the pollen
Clinging to a bee in a blossom
Out in the orchard.
And I felt out of breath,
And I blinked and I fell asleep
Like I was being swallowed
By a big old world.

AN EARLY EDUCATION

It's just an apple, I thought…
But it felt like thinking
Was hurting too much
So I started wondering
If I should just wait and
Leave it on her big oak desk
After the other kids
And she had left the room.
But when the slowest kids finally
Headed for the doorway I stood,
Holding the polished apple,
And approached my teacher
With all the heat in my throat
And forehead and all the awe
And worship in my eyes.

She extended her hand
Like she was once again
Handing me something
But her palm was empty
Except for the ring.
Then I stared at the big belly,
So close, under her long
Large blouse and thought of
The little baby Jesus
Who showed up at the wrong time
Because the world didn't want him,
Except for the three men
Who gave him presents
At the manger and then left.
And I thought he probably
Grabbed at their fingers
And tried to pull them to his mouth.

"Don?" My teacher asked.
"For you, Mrs. Denning.
I hope it tastes good."
"I'm sure it will," she said.
"It's one of my grandfather's
Prize winning apples."
"Thank you," she said.
And I saw her smile
As I passed.
"You're welcome.
It's yours, Mrs. Denning,"
I shouted halfway to the door
As I fled from feeling
Like I was being silly
And doing something wrong...
To feeling the relief
Of being safe again and alone.

MY ALTERNATIVE SERVICE

    1.
New mothers spread their bodies in linen.
Their babies' lips
Press against their skin.
Overweight maids in soft
Blue uniforms enter the rooms
And lay their dust cloths down.
They add the number of beds
To be made. So many pillows.
And the number of lumps.
These husky maids lift their lungs,
Their chests, their breasts,
And let them sag.
Using dust rags, they wipe
Their perspiring lips.
Straightening the beds,
Pulling sheets over mattresses,
The maids spread their memories
Over their own maternities
And tuck them in.

    2.
When preemies stop breathing
Nurses touch them
With their fingertips
To get them breathing again
Like God the Father does to Adam
On the ceiling of the Sistine Chapel
In that painting Michelangelo did.

    3.
I steady myself on a boulder under a waterfall;
and, raising my head slowly, I taste the water
spraying across my face as I open my eyes.

I see a body leap out of the water halfway down the fall. I watch it collapse into the pool. I see the woman's head rise out of the water. She wriggles her way up between two boulders, pushes her back against them and pushes her hands toward her huge stomach: downward.
   I don't approach her until the child's head and shoulders emerge from her body. I don't touch and hold her until she cuts the cord and wraps her child in her hands. It moves its whole body and breathes. It stops. My chest tightens. I hold my breath. I feel beads of sweat running down my face. I watch her shake. Her hands sink. I place my hands underneath hers and hold them up. The baby breathes. I feel my heart beating, and my lips moving, as she pulls it toward her and its mouth opens and closes around her nipple. I watch the child growing. I feel it gaining weight. I see its ribs becoming stronger.
   I shake my head.
   I feel sore and exhausted.
   But I stand up and start to breathe more easily as I walk back down the creek bed through the shade of the forest toward the beach.

NOTES FOR ANOTHER WWII MOVIE

after Fellini, Bergman & Kurosawa

       1.
"Crunch…"
I stomp my boots and feet
Among the rotting bodies
On the battlefields:
Spoiled meat
With blood turning colors…
Bodies, like horses with broken legs,
Are driven off in the backs of trucks
To be boiled down finally
Into wax and glue at the tallow works
To be profitable to somebody.
It's hot, and it smells
Like something is burning.
The tall soldier with the helmet and rifle,
Who is sweating, is yelling
At the others to hurry… but
The shorter one with the cap and pistol
Stops and strikes a match
To smoke a cigarette.
I watch them from the edge
Of the forest until
I hear the corpses screaming
Because their gums are peeling
Off the roots of their teeth.
I want to be their enemy
But they're really big.
They have huge arms and fingers.
I want to cry but
I hold my mouth closed
So the men in uniforms won't hear me.

2.
"Crunch…"
Hear my folks
Tramping away from the train:
Up through the trees
In the evening mist.
Their teeth biting their lips
To keep their mouths shut.
Staying together each step.
"Crunch…"
Their eyes almost roll forward
Through the snowflakes
Falling around them.
Expendable. Like everyone
And everything else
Except their own next breath.
All night long and early dawn,
They swallow the steam from their mouths
To warm themselves, and to hide it.
"Crunch…"

3.
I feel like I'm some kind of a reporter
Writing my last story…
Before the buildings fall again
And I'm buried alive with other people
Hugging our words underneath us.
"Where's my firing squad?" I ask.
"When's it my turn
To go into a gas chamber?
And when will I discover
(while I am waiting for the answer)
That I am digging my own grave?"

4.
Last night I dreamed
An upset cat was raking
The ashes in a sandbox
In my head with its claws
And now I'm listening for it
As I take another step into the dark.
I'm watching the blood
Running down my eyelashes.
I'm riding on a merry-go-round
And the atomic bomb
Explodes Hiroshima all around me;
And I dream on and off
Like a little bit of radiated lint
Lost in a cloud.

   5.
I see my father raising his arm above the backs of
a lot of people who are groveling on the beach—
hundreds of thousands—millions—as the soldier
standing over him presses his dark boot down
across my dad's throat.
   And Jesus, who is sitting on the sand beside
him, leans his head back. Lifting his pistol out
of his lap, the Son of Man raises his eyes and
opens his mouth toward heaven. Saying his
prayers, he lifts his gun higher. When the
barrel reaches the side of his head he presses
it against his temple.
   And I shut my eyes.

KOREAN WAR VET

for Francis & Leonard Tillman

Let guards drag me to a cell
In a veterans hospital for the insane
Until they send me even farther off-planet
Like the robots, transformers and cyborgs
Among the stars hurling out through space
Where I'll only keep backing up inside myself
Adding to the distance between the parts
Of everything.
Let our authorities hide me away
Where I'll be deaf, mute and blind…
And I'll dream my family's walking away
From our old ancestral caves.
I'll feel a light breeze
Bending my hair back across my forehead
And then my mother's cheeks and fingers
Touching me as softly as a flower's petals
And pollen while I watch
Her gather whole constellations of stars
In the dark nests of her eyes.
And I'll cry. And I'll feel better
After finally crying myself to sleep.
And then, because of her, and me, I'll dream
Of all the Earth's other daughters
Becoming lovers, teachers, singers and poets
Trying to save human beings.

BICYCLING CALIFORNIA

*My brother Milo and I bicycled Northern
California together when we were children;
and later my friend Bill Roalman showed
me where he had bicycled to see the
sunlight shining beautifully in the morning
off the tall buildings on Wilshire Boulevard
in Los Angeles.*

    1.

The green smell of anise
Surrounds me for a whole twenty feet
As I balance my weight,
Taking the curve in Yosemite.
Exhale, inhale. I breathe
With every leaf and drop of water.
I see—beyond the glittering rock
Between my tire and the shoulder
Of dirt along the river—
Half Dome rising from the Valley floor
Like a molar out of the gum
At the back of a prehistoric mouth.

    2.

I lean back, straining,
Bending my neck like a baby dinosaur,
To see the old redwoods in Sequoia…
Larger than T-Rexes and whales—
200 feet—sharing themselves
And their inner lives
For the last 2000 years…
Enduring fires, inhaling smoke,
Exhaling oxygen… absorbing gasses
And rainwater, thickening and
Growing runners and dropping seeds

3.
And coming out of forests in the sky,
I coast rapidly downhill
Like a red-tail hawk to the sea
Where I stop to wade in the white foam
Of the light emerald jade water
On my last legs, completely wasted,
While all the shapes and colors
Of the seascape pass me by
Like the pack of speeding bicyclists
I think of as the evening sun
Bends down over the horizon
Ahead of the dark
And races on to the moon.

THE WEDDING

Peace, for Rena

"The earth orbited the sun,
The moon orbited the earth.
Water was plentiful
And life was born in the ocean
And then on land…
And through the eons
Our minds developed
And our feelings gushed
Through us like everything
From molten lava
To ice-cold water…
And we hunted things
And gathered all kinds of thoughts
In search of the truth
About us and we began
To worship Nature and Life
Until we started to claim
We had surpassed them…
Yet only the data of the cosmos
And homo sapien imagination
Could ever tell us the breadth
And depth of what it means
To be alive and human…
And people change so fast
And often. I do…
And, with the vastness of space,
It would be wrong somehow
To make a promise
I could not keep
And then wind up
Hurting myself, or her.
To her especially," he thought.

And so, looking away,
He raised his eyes to the white dove
Flying over the blue patterns
In the stained glass window
And wondered how many couples
Ahead of them had already flown
Toward their first Spring
And Summer together,
Warming their lives:
Holy candles, themselves,
A brand new blanket
And their own bare toes…
He leaned, unbalanced,
Propping himself against
The communion rail, and
Fidgeted with his fingers.
His lips trembled; he shivered
From the chill of his own cold sweat
In plain view of all his family,
And hers; and he prayed
From the pit of his stomach,
From his soul, for balance,
For calm, for comfort—
For strength and courage—
And he lowered his eyes
To the floor… until
She came into the vault
And his spirit flared
Like the Sun across the universe
Between the pews…
And they orbited each other,
Peering through the telescope of love
For 30' to a million years.

SERGEI OBRAZTSOV

You performed puppet shows
On the Eastern Front
To get your Slavic boys to giggle
At Hitler and his guys...
To get them to belly laugh
At their own fears
Of being hurt and beaten
By some Kraut kid on the other side.
Your dolls danced the Tango
While you sang comic opera
Until your audiences felt the pathos
That can only be found in slapstick...
And yet you saved your best
For the guys healing, recovering
And waiting to die in the hospitals.
Young boys... Russians. Germans...
Who had all been sent
To be soldiers by their own governments
And parents. All having been
Manipulated and yet still
Animated enough to be alive.

WINTER MUSIC IN YOSEMITE

Are you and I
Really standing in snow
At the foot of this waterfall in the rain?
You shiver. "Brrr…"
                      "It's warmer
Than I thought it would be," I say.
And you shake your head laughing,
Arguing with me about the temperature,
As the golden sunlight
Streaks through the clouds
And enters your eyes.
I'm leaning into you like the light
And I'm getting dizzier and dizzier
As the soft spray of the Fall descends,
Bouncing off the tall trees'
Soaked leaves and limbs, and ascends
As lightly as the notes of a wooden flute
Up the mountain. Hear the water
Crashing against the boulders at our feet?
What a song we're singing.
And I'm hearing it, and touching it,
Pressing my fingers into raindrops
On your skin…
As I hold you in my arms,
Hug you tighter
                and kiss you…
And feel the snow melting into sunlight
On your lips.

THE ELDEST SON

      1.
Other relatives stand
And sit in the shadows
In her house, talking about
What they think they know
About her and what they suspect.
I know I'll talk about her, too,
Soon enough but not yet.
I'm sitting like a small child
Curled up in a blanket
On the edge of her bed.
She's blue and white.
Her flesh is cold and damp.
Sometimes she whispers
To someone she remembers
But I can't tell who or what.
A hot lightbulb's burning
My mind out of my head
But the light in her's still dimming;
And I'm breathing so deeply
But her dry breath is
Barely reaching my skin.

      2.
I place my hand on her head
And look into her morphinic eyes.
I wipe her dry lips with a moist towel
And kiss her on her forehead…
Whispering ever so softly,
She makes me promise it won't hurt
When she dies;
              and so afraid of lying
About something I don't yet know
Anything about, I hold the bones

Falling away from her breath
After she asks me for permission
And I give it.
         "Mom?"

      3.
I remember her smiling,
Doing dishes quietly,
Lifting and lowering her hands
Through the suds into the hot water,
And I see her slender fingers
Rubbing the staple scars on her chest.
I hear her breathing, whispering,
Pleading for a damp cloth
To wet her lips. Her burning lips.
I watch her lips moving.
I sit on a wooden bench
In a funeral parlor
While the mortician
Lowers the lid on her coffin
And I hear her being quiet again.

DAY OF THE DEAD

"Maria, Jesus, Carlos,
Angelina, José..."

I sit in dust, burning
On a bench in a small town
With my beret off and in my hand.
I stare at the shadows
Sticking to the laces of my boots
Beside the red and black ants
Biting each other to death
In a shallow layer of sand.
I tilt my head toward the sun,
Knowing my mind
Is still too tired to sleep.
Sizzling in my seat,
I notice the last of my khaki threads
Stretch across my bare kneecaps
Like the skeletons of *los muertos:*
La familia y amigos,
Holding each other in death;
And I think of the great oven
Of the Southwest baking long
Teeth out of the Anasazi's flesh
And the bony hands of Amazons
Holding skulls up over the boiling pots
Of the rainforest. Dreaming
Of water and the absence of pain
Hard enough to make it happen,
And failing, I remember the faces
Of tortured brown children,
The descendents of Mayans,
Aztecs, Spaniards and Moors
With gushing red bullet holes
And black eyes over the many

Streets and decades in L.A…
And like an old priest,
Tired of my own voice,
And frightened, I continue mumbling
As I recall their names.

FATHERS & SONS

Kenneth Fitzgerald Hunter
November 22, 1963 --
May 12, 2001

You were taken out
After the second surgery
And some light continues waving in my eye
Like the light through the lenses
The optometrist changes.

You rose this morning
Only in my mind.
And the writer in me is already working,
Wanting me to chisel the words:
"My baby brother.
My favorite son…"
In the marrow of my bones.

Because we lost our fathers—
Because we didn't know
How to be with them—
It was a big deal
Just to be around you.
We talked on our walks
Late at night through the shadows
In the plaza
About our dreams, our loves
And our plans for our writing,
Our children and our art.
Your devoted son, your adoring daughter,
Your lovely music. All the kids
In the audiences at my puppet shows,
All my drawings. And where
We thought we were
With the women in our lives.

You laughed, keeping it light
While each of us dribbled the ball
In himself up and down,
And alternately passed it back and forth.
You took one jump-shot after another,
Lobbing yourself up over the hoop
And down through the net.

I once thought about us
Being boys together in school
Sitting down at a big table
Loaded with platters of fried fish
And baskets of cornbread
And jars of molasses and jam.
And the teacher invited us
To go and tell our stories on the stage.
Like life wanted us to know
We were okay.

Like today at your memorial,
Like me here with my friends,
Kevin and Nancy, sitting
On my right and left respectively,
Holding me between them,
Up-right, and in my seat.
My mind pumping images of you
Through me, the tears
Gushing out of my eyes.
I can't imagine you in a coffin.
I'm trying to visualize
You being here on the stage.
You trying to sing with laryngitis.
Even to pretend
You're off the court
And still watching us all
From the bench because
I can't stop staring at your spirit

Hovering between
The empty palms of my hands.
And I can't control
My throat and tongue enough
To properly move my lips.

MY ARRIVAL IN PARIS

The plane is landing
And the windows are shaking
Like the empty little wine bottles
Rattling together on the plastic table
Between my legs.

Oh, Madame,
You taught me French
With a Turkish accent…
And ancient history
From a Liberal Moslem perspective.
You taught me how to type
Like you did in France and Belgium
So I could type my poems
And stories like Hemingway.

I called you Madame,
                      or Teacher.
I looked at you every day for three years
Like I was an art student, so wide awake,
Even in my sleep, and you were my subject.
I watched you, Ma'am,
Like I was Renoir or Toulouse-Lautrec
And you were my model. I fasted
And prayed down on my knees in my studio
Like Michelangelo did in his Vatican chapel
Or El Greco in Toledo… while my fingertips
Patted the paper with Conté crayons
And the lashes on my eyes leaned
Against the beads of perspiration on your body
Like the hands and fingers of a seminarian
On a rosary.

You called me Francois the philosopher

Because of all my interruptions, asking questions
About Camus, Moliere and Delacroix.
Perhaps I asked appropriate questions
At inappropriate times… when I wasn't
Writing poems or drawing sketches
In the margins of my books.

But my vision's blurring as the plane
Completes its decent, lands and its rubber
Tires continue expanding down the runway
And slowly come to a stop.
Paris, Madame.
                    Paris.

SPARTACUS

for Howard Fast

Forty years after I first saw it I still want to be
the gladiator Woody Strode played in the movie
Spartacus. An African, tall and silent, he
shoved the sharp barbs on his trident into the
sweat on Spartacus's skin, stopped and then
refused to pierce him any deeper. I saw the
way Strode stood and stared at the Roman
Senator in the balcony above the arena. Then
he hurled his trident straight at him; and when
the Senator dodged the trident, Strode leaped
toward him to kill him with his bare hands.
But a Roman guard launched a spear into
Strode's back. The Senator leaned forward
and slit the gladiator's neck with his slender
little knife.

Strode fell back on the sand in the arena and
died. His character died. But the character
of his character didn't. And Spartacus, who
later would lead the Slave's Revolt against
the might of ancient Rome, got to see the
depth of a man and what a slave could do
if he was free enough to act.

A FINE TUNE

Louis Armstrong blots sweat off his face with a
handkerchief. Beads of perspiration bulge and
then flatten under the tips of his fingers on the
tops of the keys on his bent piece of brass. He
plays hard until he rests his lips and throat by
singing *"What A Wonderful World."* He warms
his audience like he's a nightlight. Comforts
them… as if the whole world is a Nursery and
all the people in it are children about to go to
sleep cold and some might still be afraid of
the dark.

MY LABORS AND WAGES

I've picked string beans
With children and their parents
Right out of Steinbeck's
Grapes Of Wrath;
Climbed boulders to reach
The snowy edge of an icy lake
In Muir's High Sierras;
And ran California beaches
While pelicans dove for their next meal.

I've limped down dirt roads
With rusted shoe nails
Jabbing me in the heels,
And bled into my shoes.
I've flayed my hands in leather gloves
As I dug holes for fence posts,
Lifting and ramming a posthole digger
In and out of mud in down-pouring rain.

I've carried rough
Canvas book bags over my shoulders
Hauling canned goods,
Pencils and paper.
I've jotted down words—
And polished them to be more honest,
More visual and emotive…
And more melodic
And rhythmical like my voice…
I've spoken from my heart
Since the beginning.
I've smiled with waitresses
Pouring me extra cups of coffee…
And thanked nurses
Through the tears in my teeth

For lifting my back and raising
My head so I could breathe.
And when I wasn't speaking,
Or writing, in plain English
Like young Jim Hawkins
Or in the salted lingo
Of a pirate
In the story of
Treasure Island,
I've carved puppets out of wood;
And drawn the people I loved
In sand on a bank
Along a river in the world.

www.ingramcontent.com/pod-product-compliance
Lightning Source LLC
Chambersburg PA
CBHW031203090426
42736CB00009B/774